As a Teen Girl Thinketh

By

Mathew J. Edvik
With
Nikki Blanford

As a Man Thinketh originally published in 1902
As a Teen Girl Thinketh Copyright © 2016
Mathew Edvik
All right reserved
ISBN 13: 978-1523214242
ISBN 10: 1523214244

Introduction

Would you believe that reading a simple, thirty page book could change your life? This one can. Over one hundred years ago James Allen published *As a Man Thinketh* and that book has been the catalyst for thousands of people to change the direction of their thoughts, and thus change the direction of their life.

There is a man that you probably haven't heard of, who is a leading philosopher in business and success. He makes millions of dollars a year, speaks all over the world, and teaches people how they can create more success in their lives. His name is Randy Gage. He once said that he felt that *As a Man Thinketh* should cost $50,000. That is how valuable the ideas in this book are to him.

Unfortunately, this book is seldom read anymore. Part of the reason is that it is old. Part of the reason is that it is not easy to understand. That is our purpose of writing this particular book. To take the wisdom that is so powerful and to write it in a way that is easily understandable and useful to the generation of young women that are growing up today.

There is a definition that needs to be clear as we go forward. We the word circumstances a lot. If you aren't clear on what your life circumstances are, it will be hard to see how your thoughts influence your circumstances. Basically, circumstances are, well, your life. Where you live. Who you live with. Who your friends are. What school you go to. How healthy you are. Whether you are wealthy or poor, popular or lonely… or both. Your circumstances cover whatever is happening to you in your life right now. And this book is about how changing your thoughts can lead to a change in your circumstances.

We are excited about what applying the ideas in this book can do for your life. They have changed both of ours.

Thought and Character

What do you think about when you don't have anything else to think about? Isn't that a… ahem… 'thought provoking question'(Pun intended!)? Have you ever really even thought about what you think about? You may be asking yourself, "Do my thoughts really matter that much anyway?"

We say yes. Your thoughts directly impact the quality of your life. That inner voice that says, "ugh, I hate (school, people, myself)" or "I think I can do this" or "My hair looks nice today, I think that I now have the confidence to talk to people without trying to stay hidden as much as possible" is the biggest factor in how you feel about your life.

Here is the crazy thing. Our thoughts have enormous impact on our lives, but most of us NEVER PAY ATTENTION TO WHAT WE ARE THINKING! And then many, maybe even most, of us sit around and wonder why we really aren't satisfied with how our lives are going. Sadly, many of us in society today spend lots of money and energy trying not to think. We would much rather be entertained than solve a problem or try to improve ourselves.

It is like we are on the most super deluxe pool lounge floaty device known to man. You know, those things that you can blow up and lay on in a pool? That give you that relaxing sensation as you lay in the pool with the warm sun penetrating your skin and relaxing your muscles? The things that have a cup holder so that you can have a refreshing beverage always at your side? It's like that.

"What is like that?" you ask.

That's a terrific question. We got a little carried away in our description there. The answer to your question is this: The tide of our own thoughts is like laying down and relaxing on one of those floaty things. But we are floating in the ocean with some really strong currents. Our thoughts are the currents and because we are lying down relaxing in our floaty device, the current takes us wherever. No particular destination, just wherever we end up.

Is that true about your life? When you think about how your life has turned out the way that it has, does it seem like you just ended up there?

The unique thing about the raft that many of us are on now is that there are all kinds of entertainment aboard. There are all types of screens and access to music, movies, and books that can keep us from noticing that we are just drifting around in the ocean of thought with no real direction. At least if we end up somewhere that we don't want to be, we will have had a 'kind of' fun time getting there.

That is what happens in real life. We 'check out' of our own minds and follow our routines and habits into a life that is just going to happen. Granted, some of us have developed more positive thinking habits than others. There are some who have involved themselves in positive activities or thinking, or have had positivity programmed into them by their parents or some super amazing and perky friend. Those people are still drifting along, doing the day to day routine. They will end up somewhere good in life, but the question is… is there something missing? Do even those girls end up thinking, "I am bored with this, is there something more that I can go for, that I can accomplish?"

When we come to these points of dissatisfaction in our life, or a time when we sense that there may be something more for us even though life is going ok, the change that we seek will begin with our thoughts, especially the ones that we have when we don't have anything else to think about. All of our actions begin with a thought. The way that we feel begins with our thoughts.

> *"Action is the blossom of thought,*
> *and joy and suffering are its fruits;*
> *thus do we bring in the sweet or*
> *bitter harvest of our own plantings."*

All this means is that anything that we *do* has come from a thought that we have had first. If you are not happy with where your life is, or struggle with the circumstances that you find yourself in, changing your thinking is going to be the way to change those circumstances. It's true that many circumstances can't be changed immediately. Actually most circumstances can't be changed right away. It's also true that we don't choose many of our circumstances. But, if you want to change them, changing your thinking is the starting place. At the very least, by changing your thinking, you have the capacity to change your outlook on your circumstances and maybe even become empowered enough to change your circumstances.

Paying attention to your thoughts and connecting how they influence your feelings and behavior, and then changing negative, impure, or weak thoughts will be the force that changes your life. It sounds simple, but gaining awareness of and choosing a different path for your thoughts is hard work. That is why most people prefer to stay on their proverbial pool floaty, entertain themselves throughout the day, and stay in their crappy or 'just ok' life.

But, if you are reading this book, then you are probably someone who has the determination and perseverance to make the changes in your thoughts that will impact your lives. You want to make a change in your circumstances. This information will be some of the most empowering that you have ever read. YOU are, or at least you can be, the 'master of your thoughts, the molder of your character, and the shaper of your condition, environment, and destiny.'

You have a choice to make. Are you wanting and willing to make yourself into a great woman or are you content to drift along through life hoping things turn out wonderfully, when in reality the chances are that you will end up mediocre? When you start to choose the thoughts that you focus on, then you begin to 'develop the tools that you will use to build a great mansion of peace, joy, and I dare say, adventure'.

When you realize that you can be in control of your thoughts, you hold the key to every situation and have the ability within you to make yourself into whatever you want.

Even when we are at our weakest. Even when life is not going according to plan. Even when we feel like everything is going wrong. We have the capacity to be our own master. We have the opportunity to put an oar into the current of uncontrolled thoughts and begin to steer our minds in the direction that we want to go. It takes work. It takes paying attention. It takes reflecting on what effects that your thoughts have on your mood, on the way you treat others, and on how your life is turning out.

Nikki has some thoughts about Thought and Character:

"A person's thoughts are constantly being influenced by their environment and circumstances. A young child being constantly showered with kindness by two loving parents is more likely to pick up on the good habits that his parents have taught him, and the kindness that he was constantly exposed to as a child becomes a part of his character as an adult, and he, like his parents, becomes a force for good in other people's lives. Unfortunately, the same is true in all cases, good or bad. A young woman falls for a man who she is quickly learning is not the man she thought he was. At first it starts small with belittling comments and constant negativity towards her. Then he would just push her around a little bit, nothing too physical. But then he hits her. She knows he doesn't mean it, he swears it's the last time, he would never hurt her on purpose... Her mind becomes her personal prison that has been filled with the foreign thoughts of her boyfriend. His belittling words and negativity are now her own.

It is so easy to fall into a pattern of thinking that you have been subject to your whole life. Taking pity on yourself and blaming anyone and everything around you for an unhappy life is a cop-out. You, in this very instant, have the power over your mind to change your entire way of thinking. It's not easy. Completely changing your pattern of thought in fact, is one of the most difficult endeavors you could ever take on. Being present in your mind, actually thinking about every thought that you have, rather than letting your mind think about what it usually thinks about is hard work. It is hard work that you can succeed at."

The Effect of Thought on Circumstance

Your mind can be compared to a garden that you can work in to prepare, plant, and harvest the thoughts that you want. On the other hand, you can also choose to let the garden grow without paying any attention to it. Whether you decide to take care of the garden of your mind or not, the garden will grow something.

If you look at a vacant piece of land that nobody takes care of, something is growing. Weeds. Whatever seeds happen to blow into or fall into the ground there will grow. Weeds do not need any cultivation or anyone to take care of them. They also don't give us anything that is useful. If we don't pay attention to our thoughts and choose what we want to think, our mind gets overrun with useless weed thoughts.

A garden that has been planted and taken care of provides beauty and/or food. But there is work that has to be done to keep the weeds from choking out the useful and beautiful plants. The gardener carefully pays attention to her garden and weeds out anything that is not supposed to be there.

You can do that in the garden of your mind. You can pay attention to the thoughts that you are having and can change them if they are 'wrong, useless, or impure.' You can choose to think thoughts that are 'right, useful, and pure'. You will be amazed at how your circumstances can change when you really make an effort to manage what you think about, when you don't have anything else to think about.

But what are 'wrong, useless, and impure' thoughts? That is an excellent question. It might be easiest to define impure thoughts. These would be thoughts that are derived from the desire for pleasure. Where feeling pleasure is the ultimate and only objective. Some examples might be thoughts of sexual fantasy, thoughts of the party lifestyle. You might call them the 'sex, drugs, and rock and roll' thoughts.

Wrong thoughts are thoughts that you have about the way the world works that are not true. For instance, let's say that a guy, who is a friend of yours, finally gets up enough guts to ask a girl out. A girl that he has liked for a while, but he is a little shy and so he has put off taking the risk to ask for a date. But this time he finally gets up the courage to do it.

So, he nervously walks up to his intended date and asks her out. Her response is, "I would never go on a date with you. You are too ugly and too gross."

Harsh right?

Is he going to be super anxious to ask another girl out… ever? Most likely not. In his mind he probably thinks that all girls are mean and to avoid such a situation again, he will not ask another girl out for a long time.

Here is the thing. His new thoughts are wrong. Are all girls that rude and mean? Of course not. Is he really ugly and gross? Uh… that one might be true. Even if it is true it is probably nothing that a nightly shower and a little hair product wouldn't fix. Anyway, in his mind girls are horrible and he should stay safe and not talk to them. Most girls are not that cruel. He will miss out on chances for great relationships with great friends if he allows that thought to control his behavior.

That is just one example of how 'wrong' thoughts can influence your life. It is up to each of us to investigate our thoughts and figure out which ones are holding us back because they are based on an incorrect perception of the way the world is.

The third kind of thoughts are useless thoughts. We are bombarded by tens of thousands of thoughts per day. As stated earlier, our minds can run wild with thought, and most people never even try to take control of their thinking. Most of these thoughts are useless. In other words, they don't have any purpose or direction, they just kind of happen. These thoughts are not necessarily bad, they just don't produce anything of value.

As we pay attention to our thoughts and notice the feelings and actions that follow, we realize that we are the 'master gardener of our soul'. We begin to notice that our thoughts shape our character, circumstances, and our destiny.

Our thoughts and our character are inseparably connected. And since we can only know our character by how we react to what is happening in our lives, you will notice that whatever is happening in your life is in harmony with the state of the garden of your mind. This is not to say that your life circumstances at this moment are an indication of your entire character, but the circumstances of your life are in your life to help you grow.

We've all developed patterns of thinking that have been built into our character. Whether we've been paying attention to those thoughts or not, these thoughts are deeply interwoven into the choices that we make each day. And the choices that we make have consequences that become the circumstances of our lives. Good choices bring good consequences and bad choices bring bad consequences.

Life would be way too easy if those good and bad consequences always happened right after we did something. Sometimes it seems as though those that do good can never get ahead but that those who lie, cheat, and steal… or are just jerks, do. Sometimes it seems that way. But over time we all reap the consequences of the decisions that we make. And those decisions begin with the thoughts that we plant in the garden of our mind.

There are a lot of people who don't like where they are in life. They don't like their family, their school, their friends, their job, their clothes, the fact that they don't have a car… the list goes on and on. There are a lot of things that anyone could look at and say, "I really just don't like my life situation right now.

What we need to understand though, is that the circumstances that are facing us in life, especially the challenging ones, are there to help us grow. That is one of the purposes of our life here on earth. To learn and grow and develop. The challenges and problems that happen in our lives are valuable teachers and as we learn the life lesson that each of our challenging circumstances has to teach us, we pass through them into new circumstances. So, if you are not liking life right now, figure out what lesson you are meant to learn, apply it, and your circumstances will begin to change.

> *"We are buffeted by circumstance*
> *so long as we believe ourselves to*
> *be the creature of outside*
> *conditions."*

As long as we believe that our happiness is determined by what happens TO us, being miserable or happy will never be in our control and life will feel like an emotional roller coaster ride. But once we realize that we have control of the thoughts that we plant in the soil of our mind's garden, and that by controlling those thoughts we influence the circumstances of our lives, we then become the masters of ourselves.

Isn't this worth trying? Let me rephrase that... Isn't this worth doing? I have seen it so many times that once someone begins to see their situation in a different way, and they start to work on their character flaws, that they make progress. As the great modern philosopher Jim Rohn states, "When you change, everything will change for you."

It is super easy to say, "If my sister wasn't such a brat, then I would be happy." Or "If I wasn't so behind on my homework, then I would be happy". Or, "If I was skinnier, then I would be happy." There really are an infinite amount of ways that people would like for their lives to change. Most people want their lives to change, but they don't want to have to change themselves. The reality is that it is impossible to change people, and sometimes it is very difficult to change circumstances. But we can change in our way of being toward people and circumstances.

For example, let's look at a girl whose family is poor. She has a job at the local fast food place because she wants to be able to have her own money to buy the clothes she wants and to be able to go out with friends on the weekend. She wants her life to improve, but she constantly shows up late to work and does everything that she can to get out of working. She eats food without paying for it and takes extra-long breaks. She justifies what she is doing because, as she would say, "I don't get paid enough anyway." She doesn't realize that what she is doing is taking her further from making more money. If she changed her thoughts to trying to create as much value for her employer as possible, she would be in line for raises and maybe a more flexible schedule. Changing her thoughts would be the catalyst for changing her circumstances.

Now let's look at a girl who wants to be popular above all else. She wants to have lots of friends and she wants to get invited to the parties and other things that the popular kids are doing. She tries to be nice to the other kids who are popular, but she is cruel to the other kids and talks bad about everybody behind their backs. As a result she is insulted and people spread rumors about her. She does not realize, that because she has not learned the first principles of creating good relationships, she is unfit to have the friends that she desires.

Another example is a girl whose self-worth depends on having boys like her. She says and does things that may not align with what she truly values because having the boy like her is so important. She may neglect doing necessary things, like homework, to be able to hang out with boys. She may stop doing some of the things that she loves, like music or horseback riding, so that she is available whenever the boy calls. When she ends up not being happy, she blames the boys or puts herself down instead of working at things that she loves and that add value to her life.

We wanted to give these examples to illustrate that people attract, or sometimes remain in, circumstances that they hate, but that it is their thoughts, even their unconscious ones that keep them trapped in circumstances that they don't want. The young ladies in these examples want life to change, but are consistently blocking any growth or change by the negative thoughts that they encourage in their minds.

The circumstances that these girls find themselves in are created by the thoughts that they entertain in their minds. It is within our 'secret' thoughts that we follow our most cherished desires. Whether that desire is to be popular or liked by boys or to continually strive to do something that makes others' lives better. Whether you choose to stay in your comfort zone where life is easy or you take on challenges that will help you to learn and grow.

> *"We do not attract that which we
> want, but what we are."*

So many times we decide that we want something, but then when we have to work for it, or when obstacles come up we give up and go back to the way things were. We go back to the way that 'we are'... or at least the way that we think we are.

One example of this came when Mat was working at a residential treatment program. His team had just finished the basketball season (Mat was the coach) and to fill the time during the varsity sports class they did the *Insanity* workout videos. He would set up a screen and a projector in the gym and play the dvd's. Some of the girls didn't want to work out, so they sat behind the rest of us and chose not to get credit for that day's participation. One day one of the girls that was sitting in the back noticed the bodies of the women that were part of the video and said, "I wish I had a body like theirs." Mat's response was, "You really don't. Because if you really did then you would be out here working out to develop a body like theirs." What they had was a whim, and they stayed the same because they were not interested in exercising. We don't get what we wish for, but what we earn. Our wishes and daydreams are realized only when we they harmonize with our thoughts and actions.

Sometimes we complain about our life, but at the same time we are feeding the cause of all of those problems in our thoughts and we hang on to them in our hearts. Some of us have vices that we are choosing to take part in. Some have weaknesses that have become habits that we don't even think about anymore. It doesn't really matter. Whether our mistakes and bad choices are conscious or not, they still get in the way of making progress in our lives and for those who want to create a better life for themselves overcoming them is essential.

> *"A particular train of thought persisted in, whether it is good or bad, cannot fail to produce its results on the character and circumstance."*

This is just the same as saying that peas grow from pea seeds and pineapple grows from pineapple seeds. (Even though I have never been able to find where the seeds are in a pineapple). This is true even if the thoughts don't immediately change the outward character or circumstances of a person. If the thoughts are consistently persisted in, then they will eventually bear fruit in action.

This might lead us to look at people and say that they must be a good person and think beautiful thoughts because they are wealthy. Some might think that it is virtuous to be poor and so those in poverty are full of beautiful thoughts. Or, one might think that someone else's life seems so easy, so they must only think wonderful thoughts. Any of those could be true, but people are so complex that it is really hard to say that a person's thoughts are all good, or all bad.

Thought and Purpose

Until we link our thoughts with a purpose, there can't be any intelligent accomplishment for us. As we stated earlier, most people allow their thoughts to drift, just like the super deluxe pool floaty thingy drifting along the ocean current. Should you decide to take control of your thoughts and stop 'drifting', you will avoid a lot of heartache. Not all, mind you. We all face challenge and heartache in life, but those who drift along aimlessly set themselves up for heartache and dissatisfaction in life.

The easiest way to take control of our thoughts is to find a central purpose for our lives. When we decide upon a legitimate purpose in our hearts and set out to accomplish it, we can put our self-pity, our fears, our troubles, and our challenges in perspective. When you can really focus your thoughts on a purpose that moves you, your troubles have the tendency to not be all consuming and insurmountable, but they are speed bumps on the way to the accomplishment of your purpose.

You should decide on a great purpose to pursue and make that the thing that you think about the most. It should be something that really moves you and draws you forward to grow as an individual and to be willing to overcome challenges that come up. It could be a worldly or spiritual goal, but you should be steady in focusing your thought on it.

One thing about deciding on a purpose. There will be a lot of talk from teachers, parents, and life gurus about finding what your purpose is in life. There is a lot of time and opportunities wasted when young people wait to try something amazing until they "find" their purpose.

We are of the feeling that you can decide what you want your purpose to be and then create the life that you want. Actually, that is not entirely true… we think there is a balance to finding your purpose and deciding what you want your purpose to be. And it all happens when you get in touch with your inner knower.

There are so many people, not just young people, who are in jobs or school because they think it is what they think they should do based on what our culture tells them. We have no idea how many young people there are who have not dared to take on some grand challenge because our culture tells them that they are too young, or that they should just be interested in boys, or that girls can't do this, that, and the other. These people are not in touch with their inner knower.

Your inner knower can let you know what your purpose is. You have a unique combination of skills, abilities, and talents. You have unique likes and dislikes. There are things that you love to do that just come naturally. There are things that seem to give you more energy when you do them. Those things can be a hint toward what your purpose should be. If you are carefully listening to what your inner knower is telling you, you will be able to recognize what purpose you should pursue.

The purpose that you decide to pursue should be along the lines of something that you enjoy doing and that you are relatively good at. Actually, forget the being good at it part. You can learn to be good at whatever you really decide to do, as long as you are willing to work at it.

Mat has some thoughts on life-purpose.

> "I know that we haven't really talked about life-purpose, but I think there will be a few of you who made the same leap that I did when we started talking about purpose. I thought about my life-purpose and felt that I needed to find it. I think that I have decided on what my purpose is, and it has led me into multiple opportunities to have jobs and experiences that have made my life magical."

But, we are not really talking about your overarching life purpose right now. You might find it now, and you might decide what passion you are going to pursue for the rest of your life. But the chances are that you are going to have experiences that change your viewpoint and your interests over time. So, don't get too hung up on finding your life-purpose right now. Choose something that you want to learn or do, and then make that the seed you plant in your mind to nourish and grow.

What if you can't think of a purpose to pursue? Then focus your thoughts and energy on doing the very best that you possibly can at the things that you have to do now. No matter how trivial or insignificant it is. If you do this you will develop habits and skills that will catapult you to success when you do decide on what your purpose is going to be.

Even the weakest person, once she sees that strength can only be developed, step by step, small decision by small decision, and by patiently developing the habits of success, can grow into a young woman of strength and accomplishment. Just like someone you know who grew physically strong, if you are mentally weak you can make your thoughts strong by doing the inner work of practicing right thinking.

Once you have figured out your purpose, you should work out the pathway to its accomplishment. We know this is easier said than done, but we are going to say it anyway; you should exclude doubts and fears. We know from experience that doubts and fears keep us from getting out of our comfort zones and accomplishing extraordinary things. In fact, that is something that we are both currently working through... but that doesn't mean that we shouldn't all work at weeding out our thoughts of fear and doubt. It is true that thoughts of fear and doubt never lead to success. We can't have the energy to take the necessary steps to accomplish meaningful things when we are constantly harboring thoughts of fear and doubt.

The Thought-Factor in Achievement

"All that we achieve and all that we fail to achieve is the direct result of our own thoughts."

You have to take responsibility for your own life. For a while your parents are responsible for you. And legally, if you are under 18, your parents *are* responsible for you. In the United States at least. But, if you are reading this, you are old enough to take responsibility for your actions and the circumstances of your life. This may not mean that your parents will let you do whatever you want, but you can be responsible for the choices that you make and the consequences of those choices.

In the book *The Success Principles,* Jack Canfield puts taking 100% responsibility for your life as the very first principle that is necessary for success. That is significant. We live in a culture of blamers. If life isn't the way that we want it to be then we blame someone or something.

The problem with blaming is that you lose the learning opportunity. It is easier in the moment to blame. It takes emotional maturity and strength to admit when we have screwed up or when we didn't do something that we should have. It takes strength of thought to figure out what went wrong and how you can improve next time. We can't lift ourselves into better circumstances unless we change our thoughts.

We can only achieve by lifting up our thoughts. If we allow the garden of our mind to run wild with weed thoughts, we will remain weak and miserable.

Before we can achieve anything worthwhile, we need to overcome the slavish animal desires… the sex, drugs, and rock and roll thoughts that were discussed earlier. We wouldn't say that you need to totally stay away from boys and give up everything that you like so that you can serve others, but you may have to sacrifice some of the thoughts that you have been attached to in order to move forward.

If your first thoughts are about how to be entertained or what boys are around and how you can get them to notice you, then it is really hard to make, or stick to a plan for accomplishing the purpose that you have set forth. It takes the ability to be aware of what you are thinking, knowing what the next right action is based on those thoughts, and then taking that action to accomplish great things. We have the ability to choose our thoughts and by choosing the highest possible thoughts we can make the choice to act in ways that ensure our success.

We are limited in our accomplishments to the level of the thoughts that we choose in our minds. This is an important consideration when we start talking about getting out of our comfort zones. We can never consistently perform better than the level that we think we are at. So, if you're thinking that you are not smart enough, or that you are not attractive enough, or any other limiting thought, then you are artificially limiting your potential.

Those who are stuck in the habits of the animal mind, living the sex, drugs, and rock and roll lifestyle will have to sacrifice those thoughts and desires. For the rest of you, you may have to sacrifice the negative thoughts that you have about yourself and the self-talk that accompanies those thoughts. You may have to choose to appreciate the wonderful things about you. You may have to start by thinking of what life would be like if you had already developed the characteristics that you want to have. You may have to keep a few commitments to yourself to start seeing yourself as someone who can do hard things. The higher you lift your thoughts and the more consistently you take action on those positive thoughts, the greater will be your success. And you will succeed in things that will not be forgotten by those around you.

The Universe doesn't favor the greedy, the dishonest, or the lazy. Sometimes it appears that those people are getting ahead. In the long run the Universe helps the honest, those who are generous and forgive easily, and those who want to do what is right. All of the great teachers have taught this in various forms throughout time and in order for us to know it, we have to live it. We have to persist in making more and more right choices by lifting up our thoughts.

The achievement of your purpose is the crown, or ultimate reward, of effort. It is the big payoff of gathering the power of right thought to propel you to action. By being disciplined enough to take the right actions that have been imagined within the thoughts of your mind, you grow and become someone that you were not capable of being before. If we continue in thoughts of laziness, fear, anger or impurity we continue to descend. Even if you don't want to change, that you will descend until you reach a point in life where you decide that you don't want life to be like that anymore and then you will find the strength and determination to change. But since you are a human being, you don't have to wait until you hit rock bottom. You are not a bear that has to hibernate for the winter because that is what your instinct tells you to do. You can choose to think differently before you hit bottom. You can choose to grow a beautiful garden in your mind, anytime.

People may achieve some lofty goals but then find their way back to weakness, mediocrity, and failure by allowing selfish, self-demeaning, or inappropriate thoughts to dominate their minds again. The accomplishments that we create by right thought can only be maintained by continually practicing right thought.

There really are any number of goals and purposes that someone might go for. There really are more ways to count that people may try to accomplish the same goal. But they all begin with having and nourishing the right thought. If you have small goals, you may not need to change your thinking very much. But those of you who want to accomplish great things will want to take careful inventory of the thoughts that you have and may need to change some of them drastically.

Visions and Ideals

"Those who cherish a beautiful vision, a lofty ideal in their hearts, will one day realize it. Columbus cherished a vision of another world, and he discovered it; Copernicus fostered the vision of a multiplicity of worlds and a wider universe, and he revealed it; Buddha beheld the vision of a spiritual world of stainless beauty and perfect peace, and he entered into it.

Cherish your visions; cherish your ideals; cherish the music that stirs in your heart, the beauty that forms in your mind, the loveliness that drapes your purest thoughts, for out of them will grow all delightful conditions; if you remain true to these visions and ideals, the world you hope for will be built at last.

Dream lofty dreams, and as you dream, so shall you become. Your vision is the promise of what you shall one day be; your ideal is the prophecy of what you shall at last unveil.

> *The greatest achievement was at first and for a time a dream. The oak sleeps in the acorn; the bird waits in the egg; and in the highest vision of the soul a waking angel stirs. Dreams are the seedlings of realities."*

While we have updated a lot of this book and written it in more modern language, we wanted to leave the last four paragraphs pretty much untouched. We think the language that James Allen uses here is beautiful and hopeful. Cherish is a powerful word. Cherish, hold those dreams close and look to the future with the hope of attaining those dreams, your purpose.

Your life might suck right now, but it can't keep sucking if you decide to go after a worthy goal and work your hardest to reach it. "But I have to go to school." you might say. Or you might say "I have to work at a crappy job and I hate it." Don't worry about those things. You can still work to accomplish your goals even if you are at school or at a job that you don't like. By focusing intently on school you can learn habits and skills that are not part of the class content, but that will be far more important to your success than what is taught in the classes.

The most important of these is being able to solve problems. Having been a math teacher for the last fifteen years, Mat would be rich if he had a dollar for every kid who asked him when they were ever going to use what they were learning. The truth is, for most of you, you won't be using the math… ever. But what you are working on, if the math is taught well, is the ability to think through problems. To try something that you already know, even if it may not be exactly the right way to solve the problem. To try something, have it not work, and try something else. Those are going to be essential skills for you in accomplishing the purpose that you have set out to achieve. Even though at the beginning of this chapter James Allen said that those who cherish a dream will one day realize it, doesn't mean that there will not be challenges and disappointments. You can work out your muscle of not-give-up-ness in school. You can work on your capacity to solve problems and that will help you when problems come up on the way to achieving your goal. Don't complain about school. Use the fact that you have to go to school to work on the character traits that are going to be more important that anything that you learn in your classes.

What if you hate your job? Same thing. What if your job is so boring that you feel like you are going to die every time you have to go in? Use the time that you are doing mindless activity to think about your dream. You won't have to stay in a low level, low paying job for very long when you really start thinking high level thoughts and start working to accomplish your goals. The people who consistently take steps to improve themselves, beginning with their thoughts, get noticed. And they get promoted. And people from other companies who want high level people to work for them come and ask you to work for them. Mat can tell you that from experience. It's happened to him. If you are a teen reading this book, then you have the chance to get a major jump start on him when he was your age. You'll also be getting a major jump start on the rest of the people at your school.

You will achieve the vision of your heart. This is true whether the wish of your heart is to sit around and watch Netflix all day and not do your homework or if it is to be someone who is the central force in a great business or social cause. Maybe your vision is a mix of both. You will always gravitate towards that which you love the most. It is easy to say that you want to accomplish great things, but if what you really want is to watch Netflix or hang out with boys all the time then you will end up doing those things instead of what you need to in order to progress.

You are going to receive what you earn… no more, no less. Larry Winget has a great quote in his book *Shut Up, Stop Whining, and Get a Life.* He says, "If your life sucks, it is because you suck." If your life sucks it will be your thoughts, your vision and the actions that follow that vision that either keep you stuck there or allow you to rise. On the flipside, if your life is great, thoughts of weakness and impurity can lead you to act in ways that will sabotage your success and happiness. You will become as small as your controlling desire, or as great as your dominant aspiration.

The people that are around you that bring others down, those that enjoy impure things, or that are lazy and want life to be easy see a world of luck and chance. They see others who are successful or popular and talk about how lucky they are. They will say these things about you. But they won't know.

They will not have seen the tears that you have cried behind closed doors. They won't know that you were afraid to take the next step toward your goal. They won't understand how hard it was for you to risk being alone by choosing to avoid old friends that were bad for you. They will not have seen how you got up before everyone else in your house so that you had time to work out and/or to read something positive. They won't know that you were heartbroken when you were rejected, but that you forced yourself to try again, and again, and again until you made it.

Nope, they will just see how successful and happy you are and will call you lucky. They may even try to bring you down by teasing you or saying mean things behind your back. And it may hurt a bit. But you will have the peace of mind and the knowledge that what you accomplished you worked for. That you dug into the garden of your mind and planted thoughts of your dreams and aspirations. They won't know that you wore yourself out developing the habit of positive thinking. That you overcame the fears that were holding you back. You will hear the naysayers and will smile, because you overcame. You will know that you are on your way to the vision that you glorify in your mind and you will use this vision to build your life. You will become what you envision.

Serenity

Peace and strength of mind. This is what comes from consistent practice in self-control. Control of both our thoughts and our actions. Peace and strength of mind come when we know that we are aiming to achieve noble causes. That we are working to become our very best self.

People look up to those who have this characteristic. They are confident around others and are loving toward them because they have developed inner peace. People, in turn, feel that they can learn from them and lean on them. Because they have increased the good in themselves, they increased their capacity to influence the people around them and their circumstances in a positive way.

So many people, not just youth, ruin their peace of mind or their happiness by lack of self-control. They are on their floaty thingies, being tossed around by the tumultuous waves of uncontrolled passions. You however, will have learned to calm the waters and guide yourself to the sunny shores of your ideal life.

Special Thanks

To all of our friends and family that have encouraged us to think grand thoughts and to dream big.

We would also like to thank those who helped us specifically with this project. McKenzee Berrett, Amy Berrett, Timsy Rowe, Rachel Folkman, Hanna Gibson, and Jessi Olsen.

Made in the USA
Middletown, DE
02 January 2020

82440937R00020